PRINCETON STUDIES IN INTERNATIONAL ECONOMICS

No. 87, August 2000

TRADE ELASTICITIES
FOR THE G-7 COUN'

PETER HOOPER

KAREN JOHNSON

AND

JAIME MARQUEZ

INTERNATIONAL ECONOMICS

DEPARTMENT OF ECONOMI

PRINCETON UNIVERSITY

PRINCETON, NEW JERSEY

Library of Congress Cataloging-in-Publication Data

Hooper, Peter.
   Trade elasticities for the G-7 countries / Peter Hooper, Karen Johnson, and Jaime Marquez.
   p. cm. — (Princeton studies in international economics ; no. 87)
   Includes bibliographical references.
   ISBN 0-88165-259-8
   1. International trade—Econometric models. 2. Elasticity (Economics). 3. Balance of payments—United States. I. Johnson, Karen. II. Marquez, Jaime R. III. Title. IV. Series.
HF1379.H666 2000
382—dc21

00-063451
CIP

Printed in the United States of America by Princeton University Printing Services at Princeton, New Jersey

International Standard Serial Number: 0081-8070
International Standard Book Number: 0-88165-259-8
Library of Congress Catalog Card Number: 00-063451

International Economics Section
Department of Economics, Fisher Hall
Princeton University
Princeton, New Jersey 08544-1021

Tel: 609-258-4048
Fax: 609-258-1374
E-mail: ies@princeton.edu
Url: www.princeton.edu/~ies

CONTENTS

TABLES

FIGURES

1 INTRODUCTION

One can hardly exaggerate the role played by trade elasticities in translating economic analysis into policy recommendations. No better example illustrates this proposition than the Marshall-Lerner condition, which states that, for a depreciation of the domestic currency to reduce the external deficit, the sum of export and import price elasticities (in absolute terms) must be greater than 1. That is,

$$\epsilon_x + \epsilon_m > 1,$$

where ϵ_x is the price elasticity of the demand for exports and ϵ_m is the price elasticity of the demand for imports. Knowledge of these elasticities thus allows policymakers to predict the effects of exchange-rate changes. The usefulness of the policymakers' predictions, however, hinges on the stability of the elasticities: conclusions based on one set of values can be contradicted if instability produces other values that violate the Marshall-Lerner condition. Such instability may arise from fundamental shifts in economic structure. For example, the adoption of the North American Free Trade Agreement (NAFTA) and the German reunification may have induced economic adjustments that undermine the usefulness of the existing estimates of trade elasticities. The only way to determine whether or not this is so is to test the proposition that elasticities are, indeed, constant.

The purpose of this study is to estimate and test the stability of income and price elasticities derived from conventional equations relating the foreign trade of the Group of Seven (G-7) countries to their respective incomes and relative prices.[1] The inquiry is also relevant to analyses of the sustainability of the U.S. current-account deficit. Such analyses find that either the U.S. external imbalance will widen indefinitely or relative prices will have to adjust over time to keep it from widening. These findings rest,

An earlier version of this paper was presented at the spring 1998 Midwest International Economics Meetings at Michigan State University, and we are grateful to Anjit Bajwa and Priya Ranjan, the two discussants at those meetings. We also wish to thank Robert Amano, Edwin Truman, and Ralph Tryon for their comments on an earlier draft, Aaron Kechley and Molly Wetzel for their research assistance, and Peter Kenen and an anonymous referee for extensive comments. The calculations in this study use PcGive Professional 9.1 (Hendry and Doornik, 1996). The views expressed are solely the responsibility of the authors and should not be interpreted as reflecting those of the Board of Governors of the Federal Reserve System or of other members of its staff.

[1] For reviews of the literature, see Stern, Francis, and Schumacher (1976), Goldstein and Kahn (1985), Hooper and Marquez (1995), Sawyer and Sprinkle (1996), and Marquez (1999). The G-7 countries are Canada, France, Germany, Italy, Japan, the United Kingdom, and the United States.

however, on the asymmetry of estimated income elasticities for U.S. trade.[2] We examine the robustness of this asymmetry and calculate the rate of depreciation consistent with external balance.

Our approach, described in Chapter 2, recognizes that movements in international trade may respond differently in the short and long run to movements in the key determinants of trade. Short-run fluctuations in trade may be influenced by order and delivery lags, as well as by factors such as bottlenecks, dock strikes, and transitory changes in trade policies. In large open economies, moreover, international trade can affect economic activity and relative prices. That is, income and prices are endogenous variables. To estimate long-run elasticities, we therefore use Johansen's (1988) cointegration method, which recognizes simultaneity among income, prices, and trade. To estimate short-run elasticities, we use estimation techniques from the error-correction model (ECM). Parameter estimation rests on quarterly observations through 1994 and uses trade data that include goods and services (but that exclude factor income).

Chapter 3 describes our parameter-stability tests: in-sample tests for 1990-1994 and out-of-sample tests for 1995-1996. Out-of-sample tests are important, because they help forecast policy design. Testing for stability of trade elasticities is not new, but the literature on the subject is dated and largely focused on U.S. imports.[3] We therefore apply our current tests to all of the G-7 countries and to exports as well as imports.

Chapter 4 reports the results from Chapter 3. These show that, with the exception of France and Germany, price elasticities for exports and imports satisfy the Marshall-Lerner condition; that the asymmetry in income elasticities for the United States is robust; and that there is no pronounced or chronic instability of elasticities during the 1990s. Elasticities for German trade, however, as well as elasticities for French and Italian exports, show substantial parameter instability around the time of German reunification.

Chapter 5 concludes the study. Three appendices provide supporting data.

---

[2] Houthakker and Magee (1969) were the first to note this implication. Other studies examining this asymmetry include Cline (1989), Hooper and Marquez (1995), and Krugman (1995).

[3] For the United States, see Hooper (1978), Stern, Baum, and Green (1979), Maskus (1983), Deyak, Sawyer, and Sprinkle (1989), and Zietz and Pemberton (1993); for Japan, see Ceglowski (1997).

2 ECONOMETRIC FORMULATIONS

Our analysis uses the conventional treatment of trade flows as a function of real incomes and relative prices. This model assumes that domestic and foreign products are imperfect substitutes, that price homogeneity holds, and that trade elasticities with respect to income and relative prices are constant over time.

Long-Run Formulation

The system used to explain exports (x_t), foreign economic activity (fy_t), and relative export prices (rpx_t), all variables expressed in logarithms, is

$$\Delta z_{xt} = \kappa_x + \sum_{i=1}^{n} \Gamma_{xi} \Delta z_{x,t-i} + \Gamma_{xo} z_{x,t-1} + \epsilon_{xt}, \epsilon_{xt} \sim NI(0, \Omega_x), \quad (1)$$

where $z'_{xt} = (x_t \ fy_t \ rpx_t)$, κ_x is a 3x1 vector of intercepts, Γ_{xi} is a 3x3 matrix of coefficients for short-run interrelations; and

$$\Gamma_{xo} = \alpha_x \beta'_x = \begin{pmatrix} \alpha_{x11} & \cdots & \alpha_{x13} \\ \cdots & \cdots & \cdots \\ \alpha_{x31} & \cdots & \alpha_{x33} \end{pmatrix} \begin{pmatrix} \beta_{x11} & \cdots & \beta_{x31} \\ \cdots & \cdots & \cdots \\ \beta_{x13} & \cdots & \beta_{x33} \end{pmatrix}.$$

The elements of α_x measure the speed of adjustment and are known as loading coefficients; the vector $\beta'_{xi} = (\beta_{x1i} \ \beta_{x2i} \ \beta_{x3i})$ characterizes the ith long-run relation among x_t, fy_t, and rpx_t. For example, the relation associated with β'_{x1} is

$$x = -\left(\frac{\beta_{x21}}{\beta_{x11}}\right) fy - \left(\frac{\beta_{x31}}{\beta_{x11}}\right) rpx.$$

We measure rpx as the logarithm of the ratio between the export price index of the ith country and the foreign gross domestic product (GDP) deflator, both expressed in U.S. dollars: $\log(\frac{PX \cdot E_{\$/fx}}{PYF})$, where PX is the export price index denominated in local currency, $E_{\$/fx}$ is the price index of the ith foreign currency in terms of the U.S. dollar, and PYF is the foreign GDP deflator in U.S. dollars.[1] We measure PYF as

$$PYF = \prod_{j \neq i} (PY_j \cdot E_{\$/j})^{\omega_{ij}}, \sum_{j \neq i} \omega_{ij} = 1,$$

---

[1] Hooper, Johnson, and Marquez (1998, appendices E through K) study the sensitivity of the results by substituting the International Monetary Fund's (IMF's) real effective exchange rate for the relative price terms defined above .

where PY_j is the GDP deflator for the jth country in its own currency and ω_{ij} is the 1995 share of country j in i's nominal exports.[2] Reliance on 1995 shares means that changes in the country composition of world trade are not taken into account.

The system used to explain imports (m_t), domestic economic activity (y_t), and relative import prices (rpm_t), all variables expressed in logarithms, is

$$\Delta z_{mt} = \kappa_m + \sum_{i=1}^{n} \Gamma_{mi}\Delta z_{m,t-i} + \Gamma_{mo}z_{m,t-1} + \epsilon_{mt}, \epsilon_{mt} \sim NI(0, \Omega_m), \quad (2)$$

where $z'_{mt} = (m_t \ y_t \ rpm_t)$, κ_m is a 3x1 vector of intercepts, Γ_i is a 3x3 matrix of coefficients for short-run interrelations, and

$$\Gamma_{mo} = \alpha_m \beta'_m = \begin{pmatrix} \alpha_{m11} & \cdots & \alpha_{m13} \\ \cdots & \cdots & \cdots \\ \alpha_{m31} & \cdots & \alpha_{m33} \end{pmatrix} \begin{pmatrix} \beta_{m11} & \cdots & \beta_{m31} \\ \cdots & \cdots & \cdots \\ \beta_{m13} & \cdots & \beta_{mx33} \end{pmatrix}.$$

The elements of α_m measure the speed of adjustment and are known as loading coefficients; the vector $\beta'_{mi} = (\beta_{m1i} \ \beta_{m2i} \ \beta_{m3i})$ characterizes the ith long-run relation among m_t, y_t, and rpm_t. For example, the relation associated with β'_{m1} is

$$m = - \left(\frac{\beta_{m21}}{\beta_{m11}} \right) y - \left(\frac{\beta_{m31}}{\beta_{m11}} \right) rpm.$$

We measure rpm as $\log(\frac{PM}{PY})$, where PM is the import price and PY is the domestic GDP deflator, both in local currency.

Short-Run Formulation

Recognizing that movements in trade flows are influenced by transitory factors (bottlenecks, inventory adjustments, weather), we use error-correction formulations. Specifically, to explain fluctuations in the growth rate of exports, we postulate

$$\Delta x_t = \mu_x + \sum_{j=1} \pi_{xj}\Delta x_{t-j} + \sum_{j=0} \tau_{xj}\Delta f y_{t-j} + \sum_{j=0} \rho_{xj}\Delta rpx_{t-j}$$
$$+ \Phi_x \widehat{ECM}_{x,t-1} + e_{xt},$$

where a hat ^ denotes an estimate, and $\widehat{ECM}_x$ is the estimated gap between actual exports and the long-run value associated with $\widehat{\beta}'_{x1}$. That is,

$$\widehat{ECM}_x = x - \left(\frac{\widehat{\beta}_{x21}}{\beta_{x11}} \right) fy - \left(\frac{\widehat{\beta}_{x31}}{\beta_{x11}} \right) rpx,$$

---

[2] Data for fy also rest on a geometric average using the same weights as those of PYF; see Appendix A for a description of these weights.

Φ_x is the speed of adjustment of exports to their long relation, and $e_{xt} \sim N(0, \sigma_x)$.

Parameter Constancy

Testing for parameter constancy involves comparing the behavior of estimation residuals in alternative subsamples. If the parameters are stable, the properties of the residuals in the subsamples should be the same. We apply such tests to the cointegrating trade equations, to the cointegrating systems, and to the error-correction models.[3] We implement in-sample tests (for 1990-1994) and out-of-sample tests (for 1995-1996).

In-sample tests: 1990-1994. Our in-sample tests involve, in essence, four steps. First, we split the sample in 1989 and use it to obtain initial elasticity estimates. Second, we use these initial estimates to generate *ex post* predictions. Third, we test whether the associated prediction errors are, on average, statistically equal to zero; a rejection of this hypothesis means that trade elasticities cannot be treated as constants for that sample split. Fourth, we extend the first subsample by one quarter, update the elasticity estimates, and recompute the forecast tests. This process yields a collection of tests of parameter constancy for each quarter from 1990 through 1994.

There are different ways of generating *ex post* predictions. We consider three of them:

- One-step-ahead F-tests (*1* up): For given elasticity estimates, we generate a one-period-ahead prediction and apply an F-test to the hypothesis that the associated prediction residual is zero. The size of the estimation sample increases but the *ex post* sample is always one period (quarter) ahead.

- Break-point F-tests (*N* dn): For given elasticity estimates, we generate *ex post* predictions N periods ahead and apply an F-test to the hypothesis that the vector of associated N-step-ahead residuals is zero. As the size of the estimation sample increases, the size of the sample *ex post* predictions (N) decreases *(N* dn*)* from twenty quarters ($N = 20$) to one quarter ($N = 1$).

- Forecasts F-tests (*N* up): The test retains the elasticities estimated with data through 1989 and applies an F-test to the hypothesis that the vector of N-step-ahead residuals is zero. The size of the estimation sample is fixed, but the size of the *ex post* sample size increases *(N* up*)* from $N = 1$ to $N = 20$.

---

[3] Hooper, Johnson, and Marquez (1998) also report instability tests based on static formulations estimated with the Kalman filter technique. Their results corroborate those reported here.

Out-of-sample tests: 1995-1996. Out-of-sample tests of stability determine whether or not out-of-sample predictions differ significantly from actual trade values. To this end, we construct 95 percent confidence bands for the models' one-step-ahead predictions; the widths of these bands depend on the variance of the residual and on the variance-covariance matrix of the parameter estimates. A finding that actual trade values lie outside the confidence bands indicates parameter instability.

3 ECONOMETRIC RESULTS

Sample starting dates for our analysis vary by country. We use the mid-1950s to early 1960s for Canada, Japan, the United Kingdom, and the United States, and the years around 1970 for Germany, France, and Italy.[1] Appendix A plots the historical series for each country.

Long-Run Elasticities

To estimate the long-run elasticities, we apply Johansen's (1988) maximum-likelihood cointegration technique to equations (1) and (2).[2] Because this technique is sensitive to the number of lags included, we consider lags ranging from two to nine quarters. To select the lag length, we seek coefficient estimates that have the right sign, that are as close as possible to unity, and that avoid serially correlated residuals. In addition, we exclude systems that have multiple cointegrating vectors, so as to avoid identification issues needing future research. Appendix B reports the details on lag selection.

According to our results, permanent increases in foreign income produce more than proportional increases in exports, except in the United States (Table 1). Similarly, permanent increases in domestic income produce more than proportional increases in imports, except in Japan, where the response is nearly proportional. In addition, the estimated income elasticities for both the United Kingdom and the United States exhibit the largest gaps between import and export elasticities. For Canada, the income elasticity for imports is 1.4, somewhat above the income elasticity for exports, at 1.1. The income-elasticity gaps for France, Germany, and Italy are small, with elasticity levels for both imports and exports generally being close to 1.5.

For Japan, estimates of the income elasticites are about equal (close to 1), and there is thus no elasticity gap. This result agrees with that found by Hooper and Marquez (1995) but disagrees with that found by Houthakker and Magee (1969), Cline (1989), and Marquez (1990), who report an income

---

[1] We use the longer sample period when available (rather than a standard shorter sample period across all countries) so as to maximize the power of parameter-stability tests. We also consider shorter samples for the noncontinental European countries in order to determine whether the choice of sample period affects the comparability of estimation results across countries. We find that the results for these shorter-period estimates are similar to those obtained for the full sample.

[2] As a first step, we use an augmented Dickey-Fuller test to identify the time-series properties of the data for estimation. In addition to using a constant term and a trend, we include four lags for the change of the variable being examined. The results suggest that the variables used in our regression analysis are all integrated of order one (see Appendix A).

TABLE 1

Long-Run Elasticities

	Income		Price	
	Exports	Imports	Exports	Imports
Canada	1.1*	1.4*	-0.9*	-0.9*
France	1.5*	1.6*	-0.2	-0.4*
Germany	1.4*	1.5*	-0.3	-0.06*
Italy	1.6*	1.4*	-0.9*	-0.4*
Japan	1.1*	0.9*	-1.0*	-0.3*
United Kingdom	1.1*	2.2*	-1.6*	-0.6
United States	0.8*	1.8*	-1.5*	-0.3*

Note: * denotes statistical significance at the 5 percent level.

elasticity for exports well in excess of that for imports. Previous estimates, however, use measures of foreign income and relative prices that neglect the importance of developing countries' markets for Japanese exports. Because these markets account for more than half of Japanese exports (see Appendix A), their exclusion from the measurement of foreign economic activity (fy_t) understates foreign growth, which causes the relatively high income elasticity for Japanese exports that is found by other studies.

With the exception of France and Germany, the price elasticities we find for exports and imports satisfy the Marshall-Lerner condition. Indeed, permanent declines in relative export prices induce proportional increases in exports, except for France and Germany. Permanent declines in relative import prices induce less than proportional increases in imports. These estimated price elasticities, particularly for imports, are lower than those generally found in the literature.

One factor that may help to account for these lower estimates is that our measure of trade volume includes both oil and services. One can see the effects of this aggregation by representing the aggregate price elasticity for imports as $\epsilon_m = \omega_{no}\epsilon_{m,no} + \omega_o\epsilon_{m,o} + (1 - \omega_{no} - \omega_o)\epsilon_{m,s}$, where ω_{no} is the share of nonoil imports in total imports, $\epsilon_{m,no}$ is the price elasticity for nonoil imports, ω_o is the share of oil imports, $\epsilon_{m,o}$ is the price elasticity for oil imports, and $\epsilon_{m,s}$ is the price elasticity for service imports. Given that oil consumption is highly price inelastic, the inclusion of oil in our measure of imports lowers the aggregate price elasticity relative to that of nonoil imports. Similarly, to the extent that tourism is country specific and lacks substitutes, one can expect a value of $\epsilon_{m,s}$ that is smaller than $\epsilon_{m,no}$. Hooper and Marquez (1995) find that the literature's average price elasticity is -1.23 for U.S. nonoil imports and -0.5 for U.S. total merchandise imports, a result suggesting that the inclusion of oil lowers the estimate of the aggregate price elasticity. Including both oil and services brings the U.S. import price elasticity to -0.3 (Table 1). For Japan, the average of import price elasticities excluding services is -0.97 and the corresponding average for Germany is -0.5 (Hooper and Marquez, 1995, table 4.2), figures that exceed (in absolute terms) those reported here.[3]

Short-Run Elasticities

Table 2 shows the short-run elasticities obtained by the error-correction formulations;[4] Appendix C reports the associated details. According to the results, the short-run income elasticity for exports is greater than 1 for all countries except Germany and Japan. For these two countries, the income elasticity is not significantly different from zero. For imports, the income elasticity is 1 for all countries except Canada, Germany, and the United States, where the income elasticity is greater than 1. The results also indicate that short-run price elasticities are, in all cases, less than 1 and often not significantly different from zero.[5]

TABLE 2
Short-Run Elasticities

	Income		Price	
	Exports	Imports	Exports	Imports
Canada	1.1*	1.3*	-0.5*	-0.1
France	1.8*	1.7*	-0.1	-0.1
Germany	0.5	1.0*	-0.1	-0.2*
Italy	2.3*	1.0*	-0.3*	-0.0
Japan	0.6	1.0*	-0.5*	-0.1
United Kingdom	1.1*	1.0*	-0.2*	-0.0
United States	1.8*	2.3*	-0.5*	-0.6

Note: * denotes statistical significance at the 5 percent level.

The evidence thus suggests that, in the short run, national economic developments are transmitted internationally largely through changes in income; changes in relative prices play a lesser role as a short-run international conduit.

---

[3] Hooper and Marquez (1995, table 4.1) survey merchandise price elasticities of G-7 countries after 1946 but find no studies that specifically examine trade in services.

[4] Owing to the presence of lagged endogenous variables in these equations, the period of adjustment is generally longer than the lag length used in estimating these systems. We therefore standardize the short-run income elasticity as $\sum \tau_j / (1 - \sum \pi_j)$ and the short-run price elasticity as $\sum \rho_j / (1 - \sum \pi_j)$.

[5] With a few exceptions, the empirical distributions of the residuals satisfy the assumptions maintained for estimation (serial independence, homoscedasticity, normality). We include dummy variables for Canada to account for NAFTA and dummy variables for France and Germany to control for German reunification (see Appendix C).

Parameter Constancy

In-sample tests: 1990-1994. The first three columns of Table 3 summarize the frequency of violations of parameter stability for the three types of equations. The entries under these columns indicate whether the evidence of equation instability appears to be strong (numerous failures of the Chow test, indicated by "+++"), moderate (occasional failures, indicated by "++"), weak (one or two failures at most, indicated by "+"), or absent altogether (indicated by "0"). The fourth column shows the periods of greatest instability. The details are presented in Appendices B and C.

TABLE 3
Frequency of Violations of Parameter Stability

	Exports			
	Cointegration			
	Exports Only	System	ECM	Dates
Canada	++	++	0	1993-94
France	+++	+++	+	1990-93
Germany	+++	+++	+	1990-94
Italy	0	++	+	1990-94
Japan	0	0	0	-
United Kingdom	0	+	+	1991
United States	+	0	+	1991, 1993

	Imports			
	Cointegration			
	Imports Only	System	ECM	Dates
Canada	0	0	0	-
France	0	0	0	-
Germany	+++	+++	+	1990-94
Italy	0	+	0	1992
Japan	0	0	0	-
United Kingdom	0	0	0	-
United States	0	++	0	1991

According to the results, instability is more frequent in export elasticities than in import elasticities.[6] One reason for this result is that the data for the relative price of exports do not allow for changes in a country's openness, whereas the data for imports do allow for changes. The countries showing signs of instability in export elasticities are Canada, France, and Germany. For Canada, this instability stems from the introduction of

---

[6] Hooper (1978), however, finds elasticity estimates for U.S. exports to be much more stable than estimates for imports during the 1960s and 1970s.

10

NAFTA early in 1994; otherwise, the elasticities are stable. For Germany, the parameter instability in import elasticities for 1990-1994 points to the effects of German reunification.[7]

Out-of-sample tests: 1995-1996. Table 4 summarizes the frequency with which actual trade realizations differ from the models' predictions. Inspection of the results suggests that, with a few exceptions, the 95 percent confidence intervals around the models' predictions include the actual values. Although this evidence rules out obvious model misspecifications, we find cases in which the models underpredict the actual values.

TABLE 4
Violations of Parameter Stability, 1995-1996

Cointegration Relations				
	Exports	Dates	Imports	Dates
Canada	0	-	+	1996:3
France	0	-	0	-
Germany	0	-	0	-
Italy	+	1995:1	+	1995:1
Japan	0	-	0	-
United Kingdom	0	-	0	-
United States	0	-	0	-
Error-Correction Formulations				
	Exports	Dates	Imports	Dates
Canada	0	-	0	-
France	0	-	0	-
Germany	0	-	0	-
Italy	+	1995:1	0	-
Japan	0	-	0	-
United Kingdom	0	-	0	-
United States	+	1995:2	0	-

---

[7] Ceglowski (1997) finds evidence of instability in Japanese trade during the mid-1980s.

4 IMPLICATIONS FOR EXCHANGE RATES

To emphasize the practical implications of trade elasticities, we compute the depreciation path of the real exchange rate consistent with external balance:[1]

$$r = \frac{-\left(\zeta_x \cdot \Delta fy - \zeta_m \cdot \Delta y\right)}{(\epsilon_x + \epsilon_m - 1)},$$

where ζ_x is the income elasticity of exports, ζ_m is the income elasticity of imports, and $r > 0$ means a real depreciation of the domestic currency.

Using average annual growth rates for 1976 through 1996 and the elasticity estimates from Table 1, we find that the rates of depreciation that offset trend-income effects are comparable to the IMF's rate of real depreciation (Table 5); the exceptions are the rates for Italy and the United Kingdom.[2] In addition, differences in trade elasticities may cause different rates of depreciation in countries that have comparable growth of domestic and foreign markets. For example, growth rates for domestic and foreign GDPs are similar for Canada, Germany, and Italy, but the real-exchange-rate paths needed to offset trend-income influences differ: for Canada, the path is depreciation; for Italy and Germany, the path is appreciation. Finally, the rate of real depreciation of the U.S. dollar that offsets income effects is 2.8 percent per year, whereas the actual rate of depreciation has been slightly above 1 percent per year. Thus, unless there are shifts in the elasticities and in the trend growth rates, or unless the rate of real depreciation of the dollar accelerates, the U.S. external imbalance will widen.

TABLE 5
Growth, Elasticities, and Real Exchange Rates

	Annual Growth (%)		Annual Real Depreciation (%)	
	Domestic (Δy)	Foreign (Δfy)	Required $(\hat{r})$	Actual (IMF)
Canada	2.6	2.7	0.8	1.5
France	2.1	2.4	0.6	0.6
Germany	2.7	2.4	-1.2	-1.9
Italy	2.3	2.5	-2.6	0.7
Japan	3.3	3.7	-3.7	-2.3
United Kingdom	1.9	2.5	1.2	-0.6
United States	2.6	3.1	2.8	1.1

Sources: Appendix A, Table A-1, and IMF, *International Financial Statistics.*

---

[1] This equation is derived by Krugman (1989, eq. 7). The minus sign in front of the brackets of the numerator, however, is not in Krugman's equation, which has a typographical error.

[2] Using the IMF's data, instead of ours, serves as an independent check on our results.

12

5 CONCLUSIONS

Our analysis suggests three main conclusions. First, we find that conventional trade elasticities are stable enough, in most cases, to help translate economic analysis into policy recommendations. Elasticities for German trade, as well as for Italian and French exports, are an exception, reflecting, in all likelihood, the effects of the German reunification. Second, our elasticity estimates suggest that the price channel is weak, if not wholly ineffective, with respect to continental European countries. Nevertheless, with the exception of France and Germany, price elasticities for exports and imports satisfy the Marshall-Lerner condition. Finally, we find that income elasticities of U.S. trade have not been shifting in a direction that is likely to ease the trend toward deterioration in the U.S. trade position. We therefore conclude that a trend real depreciation of the dollar will be needed to keep the U.S. external deficit from growing ever wider

APPENDIX A: DATA

Trade Shares.

TABLE A-1

Bilateral Export Shares

From/to	Can	Fra	Ger	Ita	Jap	U.K.	U.S.
Canada		0.009	0.008	0.012	0.023	0.020	0.201
France	0.007		0.116	0.118	0.014	0.095	0.023
Germany	0.012	0.167		0.160	0.045	0.123	0.036
Italy	0.007	0.096	0.075		0.009	0.049	0.014
Japan	0.045	0.024	0.027	0.028		0.031	0.103
United Kingdom	0.014	0.083	0.080	0.05	0.032		0.046
United States	0.778	0.063	0.074	0.075	0.285	0.120	
Other OECD	0.053	0.325	0.367	0.282	0.066	0.337	0.111
Mexico	0.004	0.003	0.005	0.003	0.008	0.002	0.072
NIEs	0.028	0.034	0.039	0.039	0.249	0.049	0.118
OPEC	0.012	0.034	0.023	0.033	0.041	0.039	0.031
ROW	0.040	0.163	0.187	0.200	0.229	0.134	0.245
Total	1.00	1.00	1.00	1.00	1.00	1.00	1.00

Source: IMF, *Direction of Trade* (1995).

Note: OECD = Organisation for Economic Co-operation and Development; OPEC = Organization of Petroleum Exporting Countries; NIEs = newly industrialized economies; ROW = rest of world.

Historical series. Figures A-1 through A-7 show the series used for estimation: real imports of goods and service, real GDP, the price of imports relative to domestic products; real exports of goods and services; foreign income; and the price of exports relative to the price of foreign products, expressed in local currency. The figures reveal two features common to all of the G-7 countries. First, foreign trade grows over time in conjunction with foreign and domestic income. Second, relative prices for trade flows in both directions show downward trends, but the decline in the relative price of imports is more pronounced than the decline in the relative price of exports, except for the United States where the opposite is true.

Order of integration. To determine the time-series properties of the variables, we employ an augmented Dickey-Fuller test using a constant, a trend, and four lags. Because the test results are below their corresponding critical values, we cannot reject the hypothesis that these variables are integrated of order one (Table A-2).

14

TABLE A-2

Augmented Dickey-Fuller-Test Results

	x	rpx	fy	m	rpm	y
Canada	-1.92	-3.33	-2.48	-2.92	-2.12	-1.45
France	-1.93	-2.13	-2.04	-3.15	-1.58	-2.30
Germany	-1.93	-1.56	-1.69	-3.15	-2.59	-2.92
Italy	-1.72	-2.10	-2.64	-2.74	-2.43	-1.42
Japan	-2.51	-2.73	-2.43	-1.96	-2.52	-1.10
United Kingdom	-1.43	-2.26	-2.22	-3.17	-2.39	-2.12
United States	-1.74	-1.88	-2.47	-2.82	-1.13	-2.96

Note: Critical Values are 5 percent $= -3.468$; 1 percent $= -4.08$.

FIGURE A-1: Canada: Trade, Income, and Prices

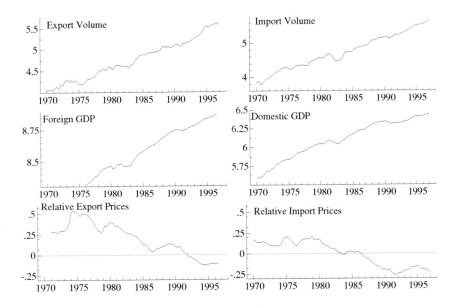

15

FIGURE A-2: France: Trade, Income, and Prices

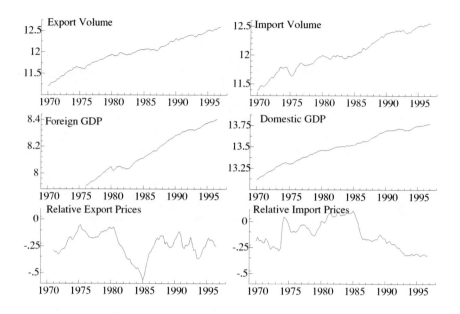

FIGURE A-3: Germany: Trade, Income, and Prices

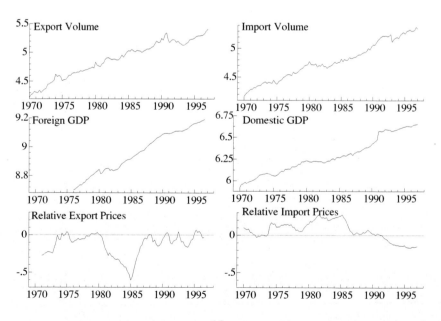

16

FIGURE A-4: Italy: Trade, Income, and Prices

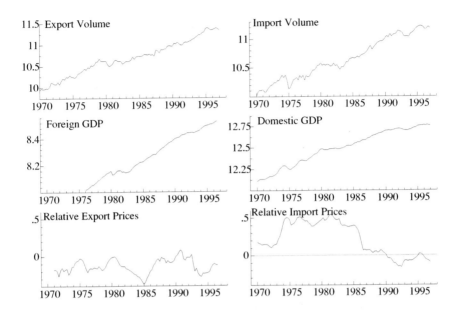

FIGURE A-5: Japan: Trade, Income. and Prices

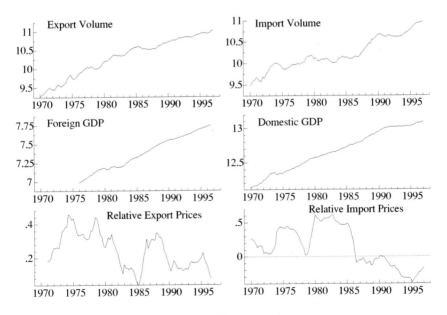

FIGURE A-6: United Kingdom: Trade, Income, and Prices

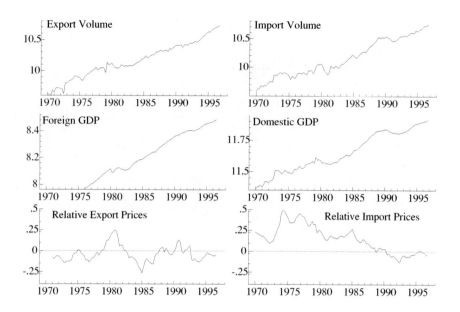

FIGURE A-7: United States: Trade, Income, and Prices

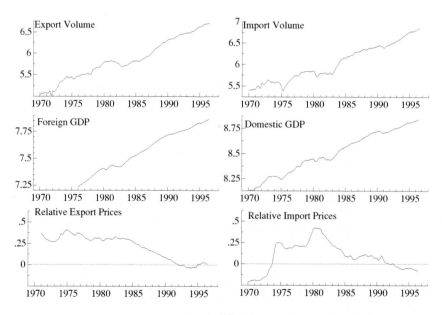

18

APPENDIX B: LONG-RUN ELASTICITIES

Exports

Estimation. Table B-1 shows, for exports, the effects that changing the lag length (from two to nine quarters) has on the number of cointegration vectors, the parameter estimates, and the tests of serial correlation of the residuals based on a test of whether the coefficients of a VAR(5) on each system's residuals are jointly zero. A dagger (†) beside an entry in the first row shows the lag length selected; "ni" indicates that the elasticities are not identified; an asterisk (∗) denotes a rejection of serial independence. For France, we select two lags; otherwise, the loading coefficient is not significant. For Germany, we select two lags. For the United Kingdom, we select four lags, despite serial correlation, because the elasticity estimates are close to one.

Parameter stability. Figures B-1 through B-7 show Chow-test results of parameter stability of the cointegration model for exports. The tests for the export equation are shown on the left; the tests for the full system are shown on the right and are labeled "CHOW." A crossing of the horizontal line at a given date denotes a rejection of the hypothesis of parameter constancy at the 5 percent level for that date. For Canada, the tests suggest stable elasticities through 1993, with a significant change in those elasticities starting in 1994. For France, Germany, and Italy, the tests suggest parameter instability starting in 1993, at the time of the German reunification. For Japan, the United Kingdom, and the United States, the tests support parameter constancy.

Ex post predictions. Figures B-8 through B-14 show the 95 percent confidence intervals for the models' one-step-ahead predictions for exports for 1995-1996. Except for Italy in 1995:1, none of the actual values is outside the confidence intervals. Predictions for Italy, the United Kingdom, and the United States, however, are one-sided, and prediction errors for the United Kingdom are close to being significant.

Imports

Estimation. Table B-2 shows, for imports, the effects that changing the lag length (from two to nine quarters) has on the number of cointegration vectors, the parameter estimates, and tests of serial correlation of the residuals based on a test of whether the coefficients of a VAR(5) on each system's residuals are jointly zero. A dagger (†) beside an entry in the first row shows the lag length selected; "ni" indicates that the elasticities are not identified; an asterisk (∗) denotes a rejection of serial independence.

For Canada, we select eight lags because the elasticity estimates are virtually equal to 1. For Italy, we select four lags, instead of five, because the loading coefficient is significant. For the United States, we select nine lags, instead of eight, to accommodate differences in the estimated price elasticities.

Parameter stability. Figures B-15 through B-21 show Chow-test results of parameter stability of the cointegration system for imports. The tests for the import equation are shown on the left; the tests for the full system are shown on the right and are labeled "CHOW." For Canada, the tests suggest stable elasticities through 1993 and a temporary instability starting in 1994. For Germany, the tests reject parameter constancy. For France, Italy, Japan, the United Kingdom, and the United States, the tests suggest stable elasticities.

Ex post predictions. Figures B-22 through B-28 show the 95 percent confidence intervals for the models' one-step-ahead predictions for imports for 1995-1996. Except for Italy in 1995:1 and Canada in 1996:3, these intervals include the actual values. Predictions for Canada, Italy, the United Kingdom, and the United States, however, understate actual imports.

TABLE B-1

Exports: Sensitivity to Lag Length

Canada (1978:2 to 1994:4)								
Lags included	9†	8	7	6	5	4	3	2
Coin. vectors	1	0	0	0	0	0	0	0
Price elas'ty	-1.08 (0.10)	ni	ni	ni	ni	ni	ni	ni
Income elas'ty	0.82 (0.11)	ni	ni	ni	ni	ni	ni	ni
Loading coef.	-0.27 (0.21)	ni	ni	ni	ni	ni	ni	ni
Ser. corr. exp.	0.16	0.00	0.15	0.11	0.18	0.49	0.51	0.78
Ser. corr. sys.	0.07	0.01*	0.01*	0.00*	0.08	0.11	0.02*	0.02*

France (1976:2 to 1994:4)								
Lags included	9	8	7	6	5	4	3	2†
Coin. vectors	1	1	1	1	1	2	1	1
Price elas'ty	0.62	0.65	0.43	0.58	4.12	ni	-0.30	-0.21 (0.09)
Income elas'ty	1.80	1.80	1.72	1.78	3.16	ni	1.47	1.49 (0.08)
Loading coef.	-0.19	-0.15	-0.24	-0.14	-0.01	ni	-0.01	-0.07 (0.04)
Ser. corr. exp.	0.55	0.13	0.48	0.40	0.05	0.11	0.07	0.01*
Ser. corr. sys.	0.17	0.11	0.17	0.24	0.31	0.74	0.48	0.17

20

Germany (1978:2 to 1994:4)

Lags included	9	8	7	6	5	4	3	2†
Coin. vectors	1	1	0	0	0	0	0	1
Price elas'ty	-0.27	-0.22	ni	ni	ni	ni	ni	-0.26 (0.09)
Income elas'ty	1.62	1.64	ni	ni	ni	ni	ni	1.43 (0.14)
Loading coef.	-0.38	-0.36	ni	ni	ni	ni	ni	-0.10 (0.05)
Ser. corr. exp.	0.58	0.70	0.64	0.11	0.46	0.45	0.73	0.28
Ser. corr. sys.	0.99	0.93	0.84	0.37	0.57	0.86	0.99	0.99

Italy (1976:3 to 1994:4)

Lags included	9	8	7	6	5	4	3	2†
Coin. vectors	0	0	0	0	0	0	0	1
Price elas'ty	ni	ni	ni	ni	ni	ni	ni	-0.88 (0.57)
Income elas'ty	ni	ni	ni	ni	ni	ni	ni	1.62 (0.42)
Loading coef.	ni	ni	ni	ni	ni	ni	ni	-0.01 (0.01)
Ser. corr. exp.	0.09	0.04*	0.73	0.93	0.76	0.73	0.51	0.66
Ser. corr. sys.	0.30	0.14	0.30	0.34	0.53	0.83	0.88	0.97

Japan (1977:2 to 1994:4)

Lags included	9	8	7	6	5†	4	3	2
Coin. vectors	1	0	0	0	1	1	1	0
Price elas'ty	1.31	ni	ni	ni	-1.01 (0.12)	-1.51	-1.32	ni
Income elas'ty	1.21	ni	ni	ni	1.12 (0.06)	0.66	0.94	ni
Loading coef.	-0.04	ni	ni	ni	-0.13 (0.08)	-0.00	-0.02	ni
Ser. corr. exp.	0.00*	0.00*	0.02*	0.81	0.16	0.21	0.25	0.04*
Ser. corr. sys.	0.01*	0.00*	0.00*	0.27	0.51	0.70	0.73	0.14

United Kingdom (1977:1 to 1994:4)

Lags included	9	8	7	6	5	4†	3	2
Coin. vectors	1	1	1	1	1	1	1	1
Price elas'ty	1.17	0.60	0.49	0.88	1.06	-1.55 (0.51)	-3.41	-1.02
Income elas'ty	0.96	1.11	1.18	1.16	1.16	1.11 (0.32)	1.18	2.28
Loading coef.	0.18	0.30	0.25	0.04	0.03	-0.02 (0.02)	-0.08	-0.06
Ser. corr. exp.	0.84	0.55	0.12	0.05	0.27	0.00*	0.18	0.37
Ser. corr. sys.	0.90	0.74	0.50	0.16	0.17	0.00*	0.00*	0.00*

United States (1976:3 to 1994:4)

Lags included	9	8	7	6	5	4	3	2†
Coin. vectors	2	2	1	1	1	0	0	1
Price elas'ty	ni	ni	-1.38	-1.44	-1.51	ni	ni	-1.47 (0.24)
Income elas'ty	ni	ni	0.89	0.73	0.74	ni	ni	0.83 (0.19)
Loading coef.	ni	ni	-0.15	0.03	-0.05	ni	ni	-0.06 (0.05)
Ser. corr. exp.	0.50	0.28	0.09	0.14	0.06	0.64	0.97	0.81
Ser. corr. sys.	0.27	0.01*	0.00*	0.00*	0.01*	0.05	0.84	0.71

TABLE B-2
Imports: Sensitivity to Lag Length

				Canada (1963:1 to 1994:4)				
Lags included	9	8†	7	6	5	4	3	2
Coin. vectors	0	1	0	1	1	1	1	1
Price elas'ty	ni	-1.01 (0.17)	ni	-0.83	3.35	-2.83	-17.33	0.33
Income elas'ty	ni	-1.36 (0.07)	ni	1.24	0.74	1.60	4.02	1.17
Loading coef.	ni	-0.20 (0.05)	ni	-0.06	-0.00	-0.01	0.00	-0.01
Ser. corr. imp.	0.25	0.04*	0.16	0.15	0.36	0.11	0.08	0.55
Ser. corr. sys.	0.60	0.14	0.30	0.53	0.58	0.51	0.25	0.13

				France (1972:2 to 1994:4)				
Lags included	9	8	7	6	5	4	3†	2
Coin. vectors	0	0	0	0	0	1	1	1
Price elas'ty	ni	ni	ni	ni	ni	-0.35	-0.37 (0.03)	-0.38
Income elas'ty	ni	ni	ni	ni	ni	1.61	1.59 (0.03)	1.59
Loading coef.	ni	ni	ni	ni	ni	-0.61	-0.60 (0.03)	-0.47
Ser. corr. imp.	0.00*	0.02*	0.08*	0.32	0.16	0.18	0.08	0.03
Ser. corr. sys.	0.09	0.17	0.07	0.00*	0.10	0.02*	0.12	0.01*

				Germany (1968:3 to 1994:4)				
Lags included	9	8	7	6	5	4	3	2†
Coin. vectors	2	0	1	0	0	0	1	1
Price elas'ty	ni	ni	0.25	ni	ni	ni	0.31	-0.06 (0.23)
Income elas'ty	ni	ni	1.65	ni	ni	ni	1.63	1.47 (0.13)
Loading coef.	ni	ni	-0.10	ni	ni	ni	0.07	-0.13 (0.02)
Ser. corr. imp.	0.31	0.01*	0.18	0.05	0.31	0.02*	0.03*	0.05
Ser. corr. sys.	0.74	0.31	0.29	0.27	0.31	0.18	0.17	0.00*

				Italy (1972:2 to 1994:4)				
Lags included	9	8	7	6	5	4†	3	2
Coin. vectors	2	2	2	2	1	1	1	1
Price elas'ty	ni	ni	ni	ni	-0.63	-0.40 (0.04)	-0.39	-0.39
Income elas'ty	ni	ni	ni	ni	0.78	1.40 (0.05)	1.42	1.42
Loading coef.	ni	ni	ni	ni	-0.06	-0.50 (0.12)	-0.53	-0.48
Ser. corr. imp.	0.46	0.54	0.83	0.77	0.17	0.82	0.88	0.73
Ser. corr. sys.	0.16	0.07	0.22	0.48	0.17	0.11	0.02*	0.02*

				Japan (1956:4 to 1994:4)				
Lags included	9	8	7	6†	5	4	3	2
Coin. vectors	2	2	2	1	2	2	2	2
Price elas'ty	ni	ni	ni	-0.33 (0.21)	ni	ni	ni	ni
Income elas'ty	ni	ni	ni	0.92 (0.12)	ni	ni	ni	ni
Loading coef.	ni	ni	ni	-0.03 (0.01)	ni	ni	ni	ni
Ser. corr. imp.	0.60	0.36	0.63	0.22	0.10	0.00*	0.00*	0.01*
Ser. corr. sys.	0.22	0.12	0.27	0.03*	0.26	0.00*	0.00*	0.00*

22

United Kingdom (1956:2 to 1994:4)							
Lags included	9	8	7	6	5†	4	3	2
Coin. vectors	0	0	0	0	1	2	2	2
Price elas'ty	ni	ni	ni	ni	-0.58 (1.50)	ni	ni	ni
Income elas'ty	ni	ni	ni	ni	2.21 (0.82)	ni	ni	ni
Loading coef.	ni	ni	ni	ni	0.01 (0.01)	ni	ni	ni
Ser. corr. imp.	0.31	0.63	0.72	0.20	0.33	0.44	0.67	0.90
Ser. corr. sys.	0.41	0.16	0.41	0.05	0.13	0.06	0.46	0.35
United States (1961:4 to 1994:4)							
Lags included	9†	8	7	6	5	4	3	2
Coin. vectors	1	1	1	1	1	1	1	1
Price elas'ty	-0.31 (0.09)	-0.21	-0.37	-0.36	-0.41	-0.43	ni	ni
Income elas'ty	1.79 (0.15)	1.72	2.76	2.12	2.10	2.10	ni	ni
Loading coef.	-0.10 (0.03)	-0.08	0.01	0.01	-0.03	-0.03	ni	ni
Ser. corr. imp.	0.12	0.37	0.11	0.03*	0.31	0.37	0.06	0.81
Ser. corr. sys.	0.26	0.12	0.02*	0.02*	0.03*	0.02*	0.00*	0.00*

FIGURE B-1: Exports for Canada: Chow Tests for the Cointegration Model

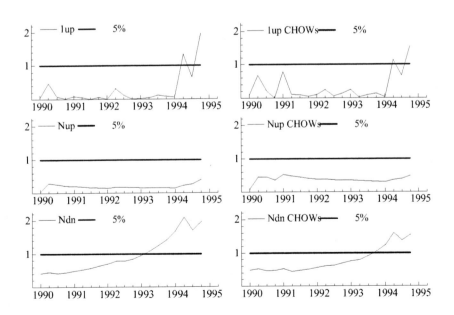

FIGURE B-2: Exports for France: Chow Tests for the Cointegration Model

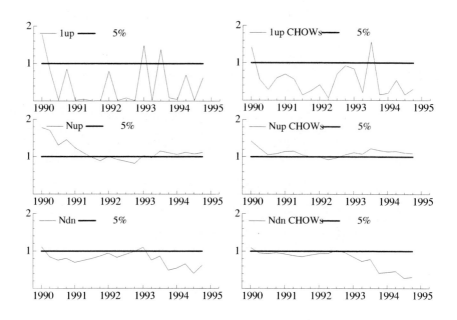

FIGURE B-3: Exports for Germany: Chow Tests for the Cointegration Model

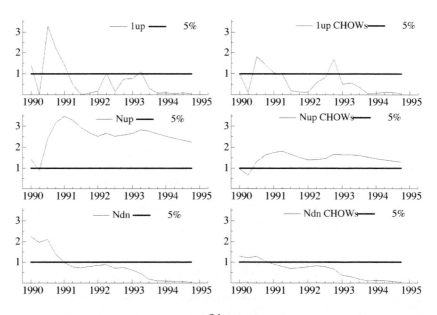

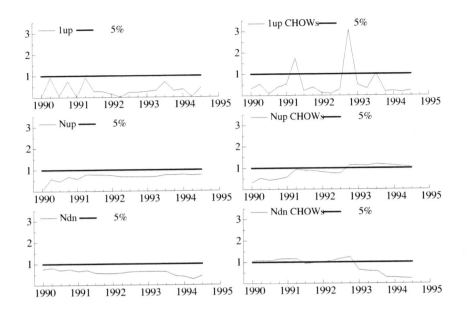

FIGURE B-4: Exports for Italy: Chow Tests for the Cointegration Model

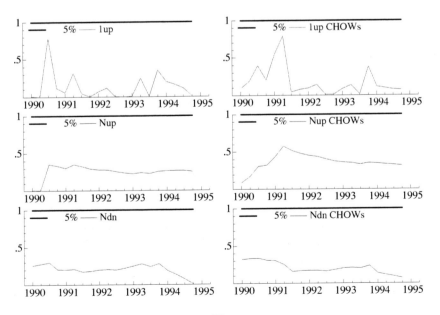

FIGURE B-5: Exports for Japan: Chow Tests for the Cointegration Model

FIGURE B-6: Exports for the U.K.: Chow Tests for the Cointegration Model

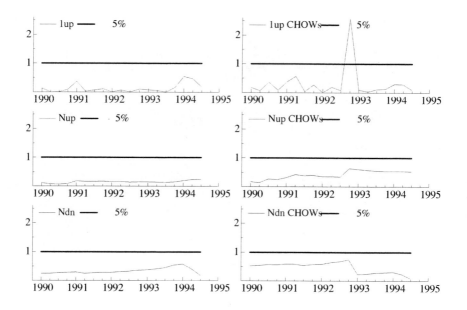

FIGURE B-7: Exports for the U.S.: Chow Tests for the Cointegration Model

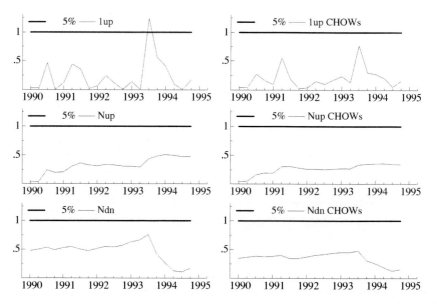

FIGURE B-8: Exports for Canada: Predictive Accuracy of the Cointegration Model

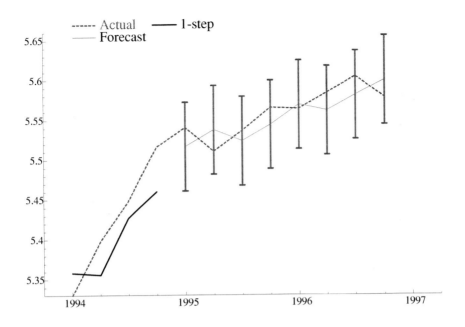

FIGURE B-9: Exports for France: Predictive Accuracy of the Cointegration Model

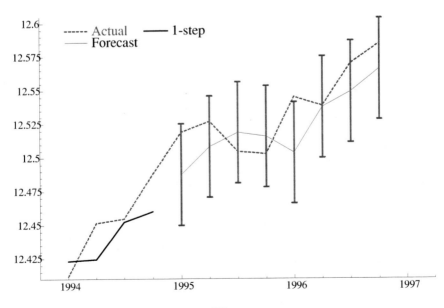

FIGURE B-10: Exports for Germany: Predictive Accuracy of the Cointegration Model

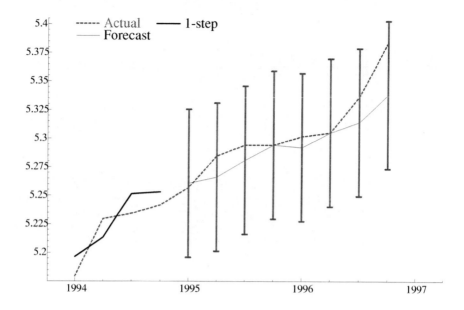

FIGURE B-11: Exports for Italy: Predictive Accuracy of the Cointegration Model

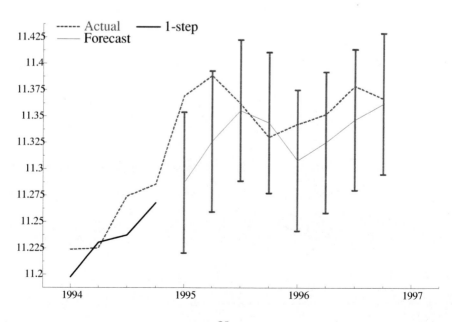

FIGURE B-12: Exports for Japan: Predictive Accuracy of the Cointegration Model

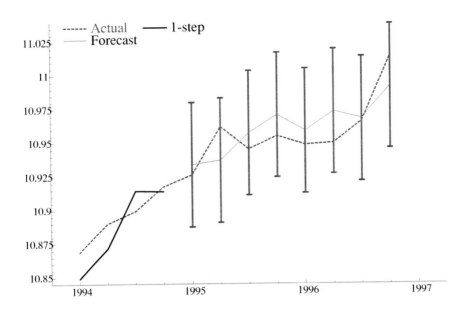

FIGURE B-13: Exports for the U.K.: Predictive Accuracy of the Cointegration Model

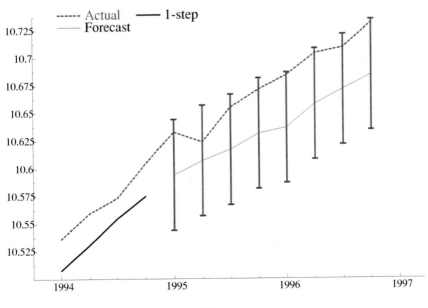

FIGURE B-14: Exports for the U.S.: Predictive Accuracy of the Cointegration Model

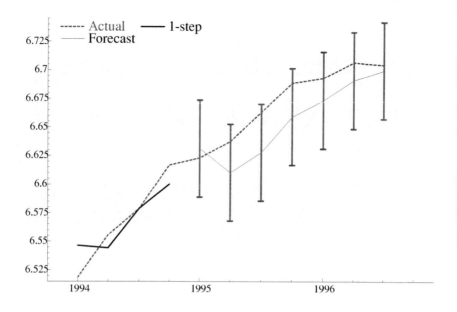

FIGURE B-15: Imports for Canada: Chow Tests for the Cointegration Model

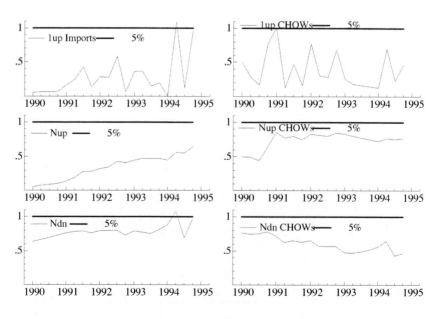

FIGURE B-16: Imports for France: Chow Tests for the Cointegration Model

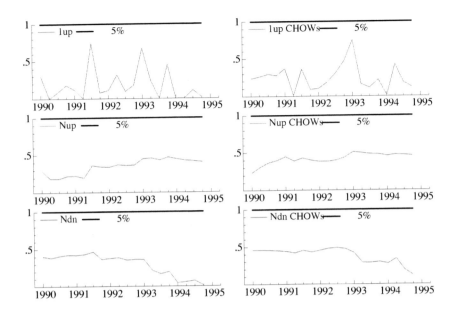

FIGURE B-17: Imports for Germany: Chow Tests for the Cointegration Model

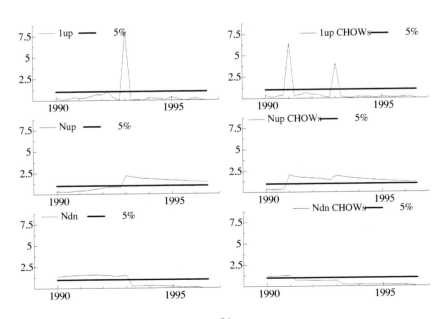

FIGURE B-18: Imports for Italy: Chow Tests for the Cointegration Model

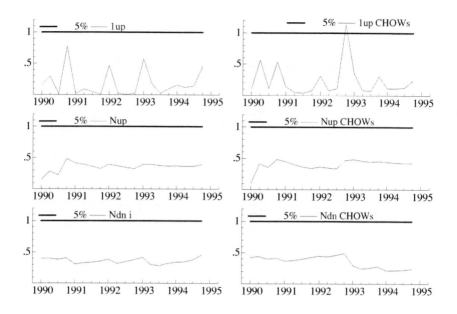

FIGURE B-19: Imports for Japan: Chow Tests for the Cointegration Model

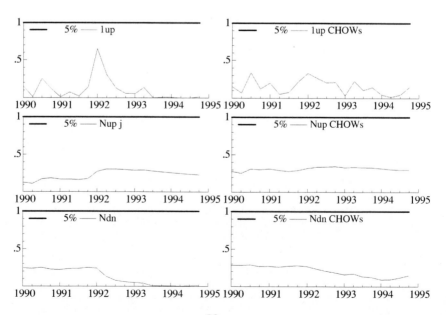

FIGURE B-20: Imports for the U.K.: Chow Tests for the Cointegration Model

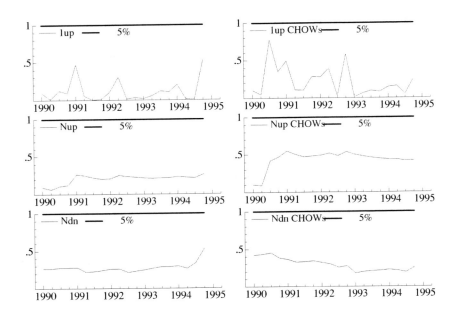

FIGURE B-21: Imports for the U.S.: Chow Tests for the Cointegration Model

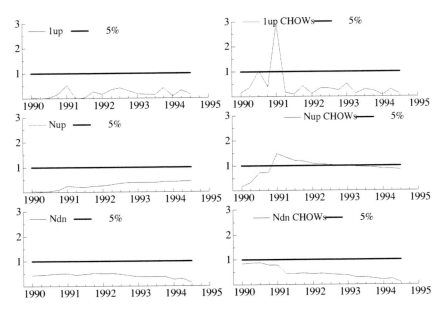

FIGURE B-22: Imports for Canada: Predictive Accuracy of the Cointegration Model

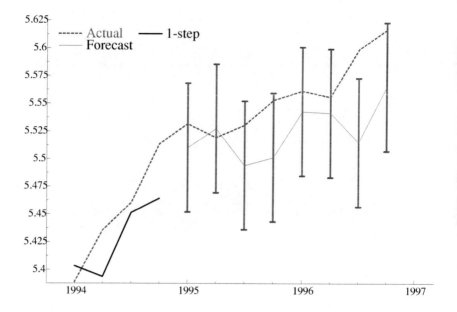

FIGURE B-23: Imports for France: Predictive Accuracy of the Cointegration Model

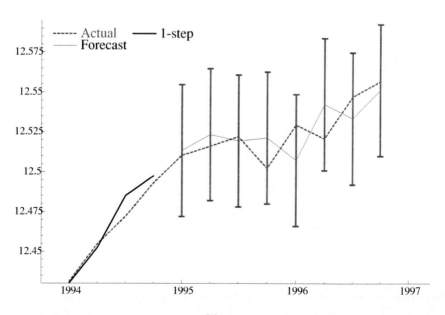

FIGURE B-24: Imports for Germany: Predictive Accuracy of the Cointegration Model

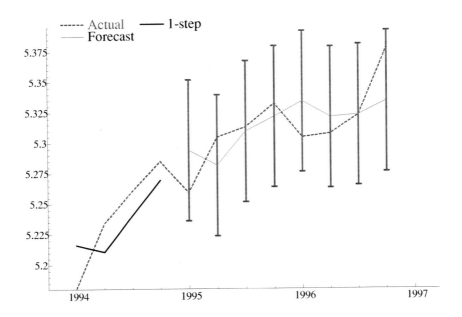

FIGURE B-25: Imports for Italy: Predictive Accuracy of the Cointegration Model

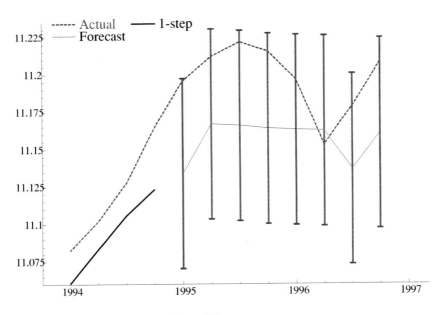

FIGURE B-26: Imports for Japan: Predictive Accuracy of the Cointegration Model

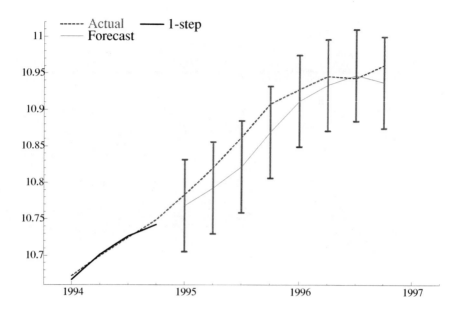

FIGURE B-27: Imports for the U.K.: Predictive Accuracy of the Cointegration Model

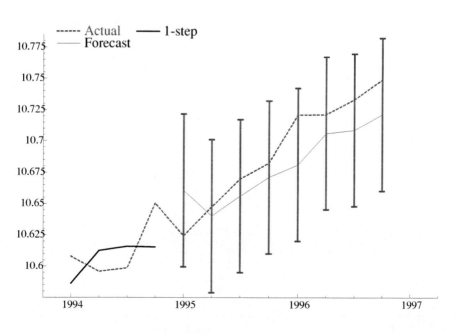

FIGURE B-28: Imports for the U.S.: Predictive Accuracy of the Cointegration Model

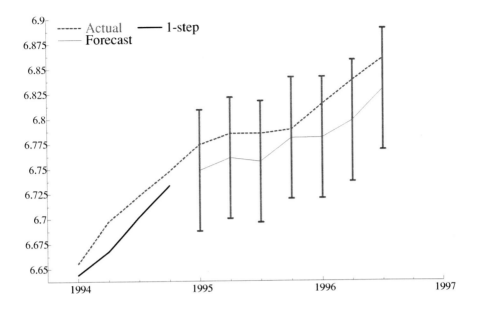

APPENDIX C: SHORT-RUN ELASTICITIES

Exports

Estimation. Table C-1 shows, for exports, that all of the coefficients have their expected signs and that countries differ markedly in their estimated adjustment speeds, ranging from 3 percent per quarter (United Kingdom) to 48 percent per quarter (Germany). The error-correction coefficient for France, Italy, and the United States is not significant, a finding that weakens the evidence on cointegration.

TABLE C-1

Exports: Parameter Estimates from the Error-Correction Model

	Can	Fra	Ger	Ita	Jap	U.K.	U.S.
Income	1.07	1.82	0.55	2.33	0.59	1.09	1.83
	(0.34)	(0.43)	(0.41)	(0.60)	(0.34)	(0.65)	(0.48)
Price	-0.48	-0.09	-0.05	-0.33	-0.45	-0.24	-0.53
	(0.15)	(0.06)	(0.06)	(0.13)	(0.12)	(0.10)	(0.23)
ECM	-0.20	-0.01	-0.48	-0.03	-0.17	-0.03	-0.05
	(0.08)	(0.04)	(0.07)	(0.04)	(0.06)	(0.01)	(0.05)
R^2	0.51	0.52	0.57	0.33	0.49	0.74	0.49
SER	2.51	1.69	2.30	3.34	2.04	1.18	1.79
Serial indep'nce	0.25	0.21	0.19	0.48	0.06	0.06	0.18
Homoscedas'ty	0.07	0.84	0.50	0.19	0.99	0.69	0.50
Normality	0.53	0.78	0.09	0.23	0.93	0.41	0.49
Functional form	0.90	0.82	0.06	0.76	0.87	0.87	0.06
Start sample	76.2	76.3	76.2	76.3	77.3	77.3	76.3

Note: Standard errors are in parentheses.

The formulations explain at least one-half of the variability of the growth rate of exports, except for Italy, where they explain about one-third. Finally, the empirical distributions of the residuals satisfy the assumptions maintained for estimation (serial independence, homoscedasticity, normality) in all cases. For homoscedasticity, we use a t-test of the null hypothesis that the variance of the residuals is constant. For normality, we use a χ^2 test of the null hypothesis that the distribution of the residuals is normal. For functional form, we use a reset test of the null hypothesis that the specification does not omit combinations of the predetermined variables.

38

Some formulations include dummy variables: Canada (1994:1) includes a variable for NAFTA; France (1990:1&2) and Germany (1990:1,3,4) include a variable for the effects of German reunification; the United Kingdom (1979:1&2) and the United States (1978:2; 1977:4) include a variable for oil-price shocks.

Parameter stability. Figures C-1 through C-7 show Chow tests of parameter stability for exports. For Canada, France, Japan, and the United Kingdom, the tests support parameter constancy. For Germany and the United States, they show evidence of some instability.

Ex post predictions. Figures C-8 through C-14 show the 95 percent confidence intervals for the models' one-step-ahead predictions for exports for 1995-1996. Except for Italy in 1995:1 and the United States in 1995:2, the actual values are in the 95 percent confidence intervals. Predictions for Germany, the United Kingdom, and the United States, however, are one-sided.

FIGURE C-1: Exports for Canada: Chow Tests for the ECM Coefficients

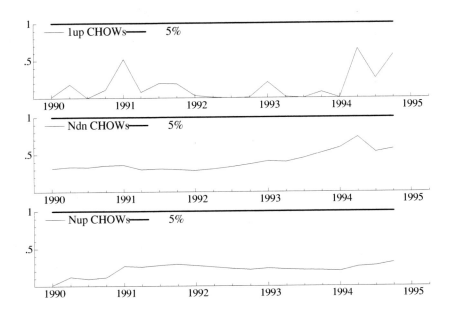

FIGURE C-2: Exports for France: Chow Tests for the ECM Coefficients

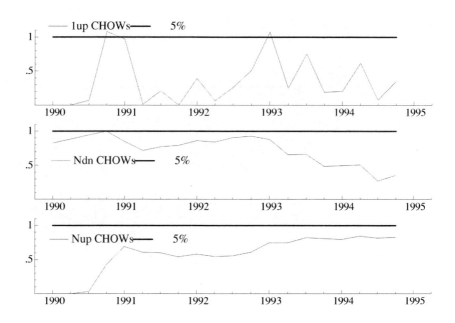

FIGURE C-3: Exports for Germany: Chow Tests for the ECM Coefficients

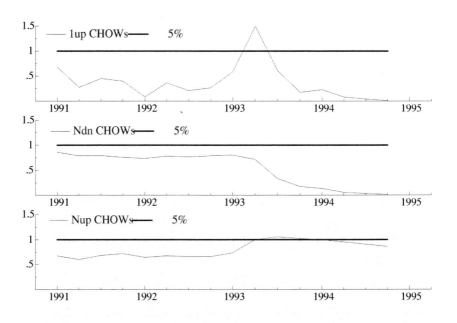

FIGURE C-4: Exports for Italy: Chow Tests for the ECM Coefficients

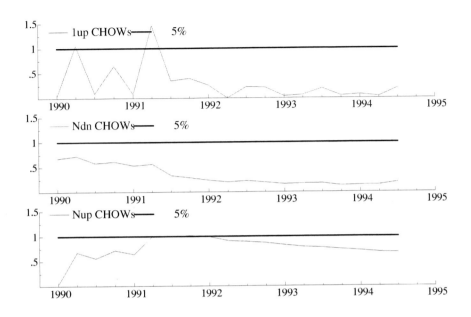

FIGURE C-5: Exports for Japan: Chow Tests for the ECM Coefficients

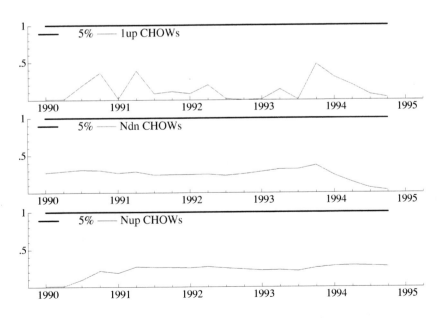

41

FIGURE C-6: Exports for the U.K.: Chow Tests for the ECM Coefficients

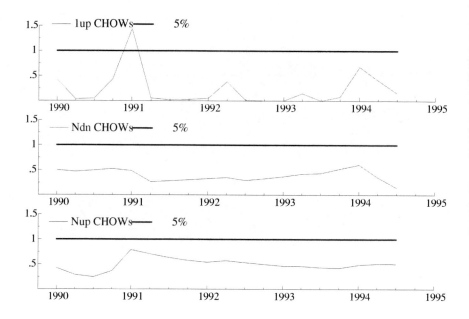

FIGURE C-7: Exports for the U.S.: Chow Tests for the ECM Coefficients

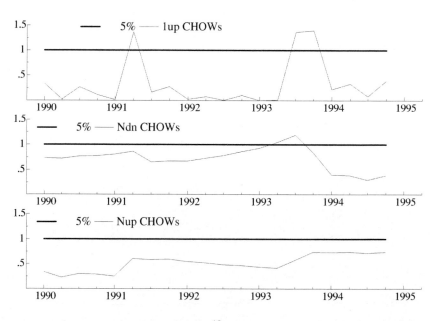

FIGURE C-8: Exports for Canada: Predictive Accuracy of the Error-Correction Model

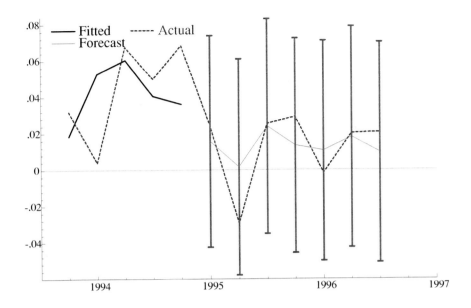

FIGURE C-9: Exports for France: Predictive Accuracy of the Error-Correction Model

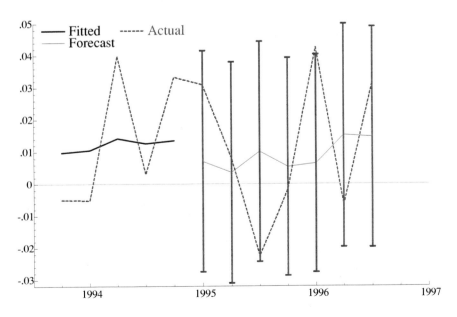

FIGURE C-10: Exports for Germany Predictive Accuracy of the Error-Correction Model

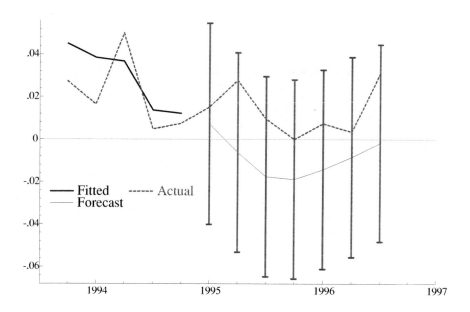

FIGURE C-11: Exports for Italy: Predictive Accuracy of the Error-Correction Model

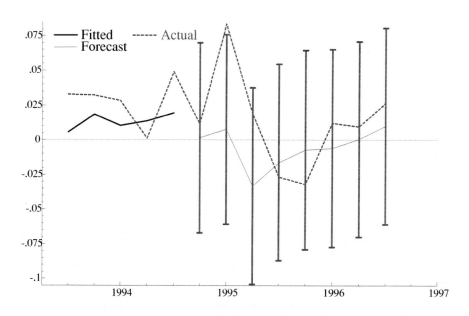

FIGURE C-12: Exports for Japan: Predictive Accuracy of the Error-Correction Model

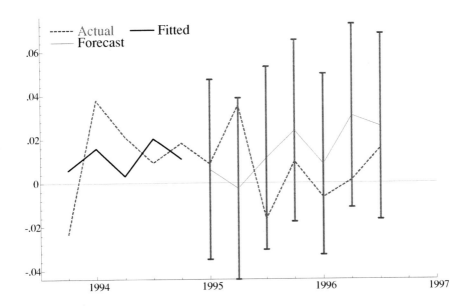

FIGURE C-13: Exports for the U.K.: Predictive Accuracy of the Error-Correction Model

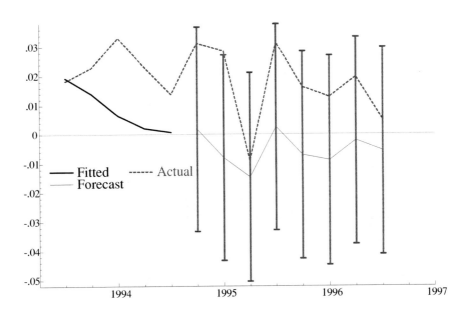

FIGURE C-14: Exports for the U.S. Predictive Accuracy of the Error-Correction Model

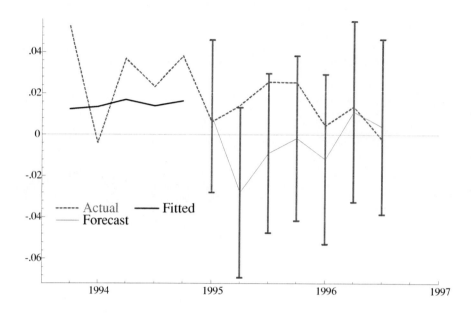

Imports

   Estimation. Table C-2 shows, for imports, that all the coefficients have their expected signs and that countries differ markedly in their estimated adjustment speeds, which range from 2 percent per quarter (United Kingdom) to 36 percent per quarter (Italy). The error-correction coefficient is significant for all countries, except the United States, a finding that weakens the evidence on cointegration. The formulations differ in their ability to explain the variability of the growth rate of imports, which ranged from 23 percent for the United Kingdom to 67 percent for France. Finally, the empirical distributions of the residuals satisfy the assumptions maintained for estimation (serial independence, homoscedasticity, normality), except for Canada (normality) and the United Kingdom (homoscedasticity and normality).

   Some formulations include dummy variables: Canada includes a dummy variable for NAFTA that takes a value of 1 starting in 1994:1; Germany (1993:1) includes a variable for the ERM crisis; Japan (1972:1; 1989:1) and the United Kingdom (1972:4; 1975:2; 1979:4) include a variable for oil-price shocks; and the United States (1969:1&2; 1972:1&2; 1974:2) includes variables for dock strikes and price controls.

Parameter stability. Figures C-15 through C-21 show Chow tests for imports pointing to a remarkable degree of parameter constancy across countries.

Ex post predictions. Figures C-22 through C-28 show the 95 percent confidence intervals for the models' one-step-ahead predictions for imports for 1995-1996. Except for Japan in 1995:2, the actual values for these predictions fall within the 95 percent confidence intervals. Predictions for Canada and France, however, understate the growth rates for imports.

TABLE C-2

Imports: Parameter Estimates of the Error-Correction Model

	Can	Fra	Ger	Ita	Jap	U.K.	U.S.
Income	1.26	1.65	0.99	1.01	1.00	1.01	2.31
	(0.21)	(0.40)	(0.25)	(0.37)	(0.37)	(0.30)	(0.30)
Price	-0.14	-0.06	-0.17	–	-0.05	–	-0.55
	(0.16)	(0.14)	(0.08)		(0.09)		(0.14)
ECM	-0.11	-0.34	-0.10	-0.36	-0.04	-0.02	-0.04
	(0.04)	(0.07)	(0.02)	(0.06)	(0.02)	(0.01)	(0.03)
R^2	0.44	0.67	0.49	0.42	0.52	0.23	0.63
SER	2.77	1.63	2.32	3.02	2.91	2.91	2.48
Serial correl'tn	0.97	0.21	0.42	0.08	0.28	0.05	0.30
Homoscedas'ty	0.79	0.24	0.83	0.56	0.21	0.02*	0.08
Normality	0.01*	0.74	0.96	0.34	0.57	0.00*	0.12
Functonal form	0.38	0.51	0.02*	0.04*	0.09	0.78	0.35
Start sample	61.2	71.3	68.3	70.3	56.4	55.4	60.3

Note: Standard errors are in parentheses; * denotes statistical significance at the 5 percent level.

FIGURE C-15: Imports for Canada: Chow Tests for the ECM Coefficients

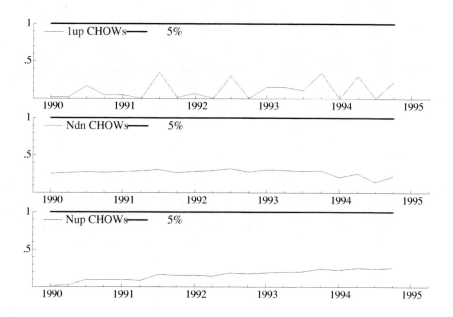

FIGURE C-16: Imports for France: Chow Tests for the ECM Coefficients

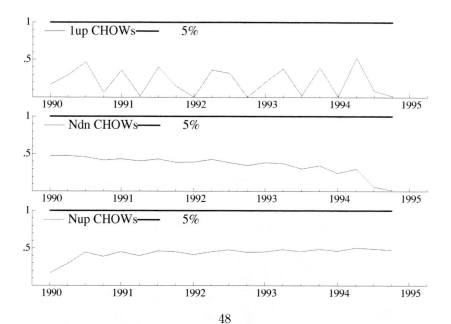

48

FIGURE C-17: Imports for Germany: Chow Tests for the ECM Coefficients

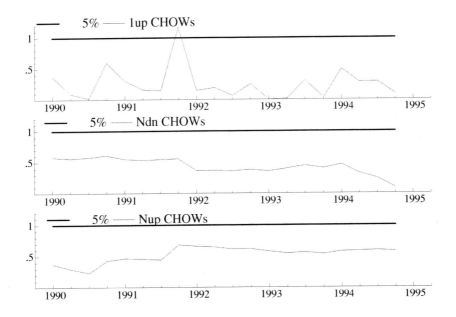

FIGURE C-18: Imports for Italy: Chow Tests for the ECM Coefficients

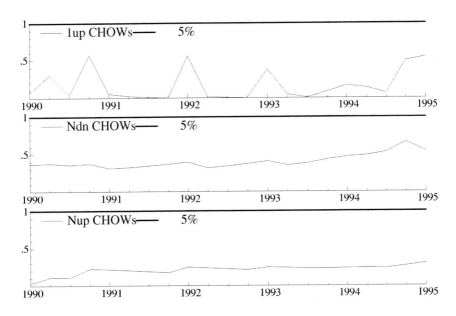

FIGURE C-19: Imports for Japan: Chow Tests for the ECM Coefficients

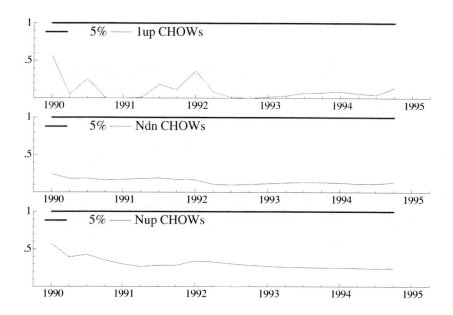

FIGURE C-20: Imports for the U.K.: Chow Tests for the ECM Coefficients

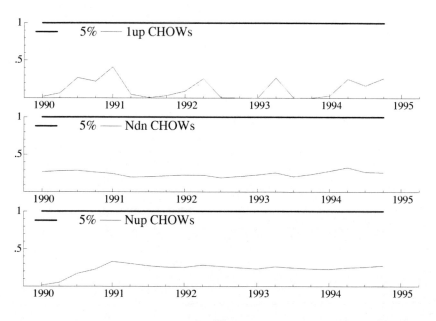

FIGURE C-21: Imports for the U.S.: Chow Tests for the ECM Coefficients

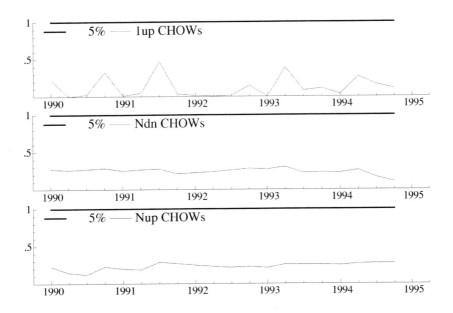

FIGURE C-22: Imports for Canada: Predictive Accuracy of the Error-Correction Model

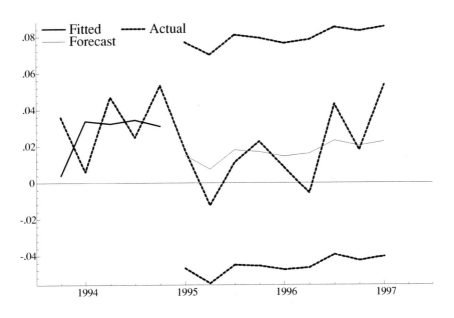

FIGURE C-23: Imports for France: Predictive Accuracy of the Error-Correction Model

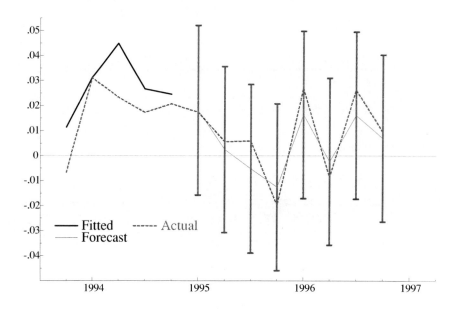

FIGURE C-24: Imports for Germany: Predictive Accuracy of the Error-Correction Model

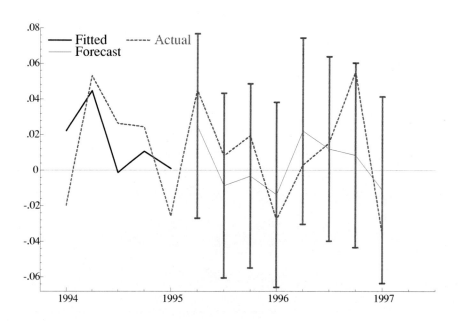

FIGURE C-25: Imports for Italy: Predictive Accuracy of the Error-Correction Model

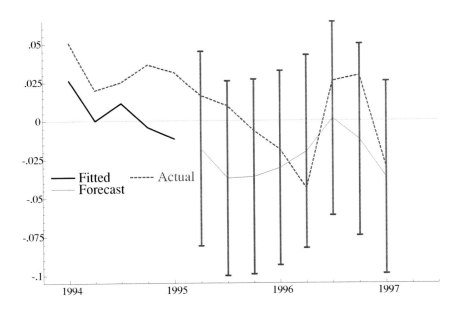

FIGURE C-26: Imports for Japan: Predictive Accuracy of the Error-Correction Model

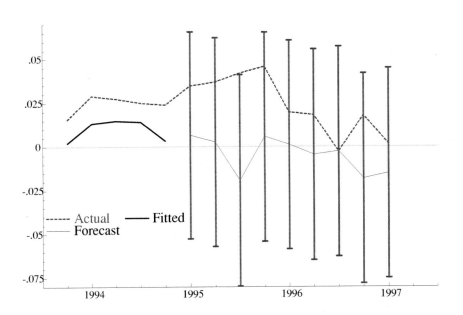

FIGURE C-27: Imports for the U.K.: Predictive Accuracy of the Error-Correction Model

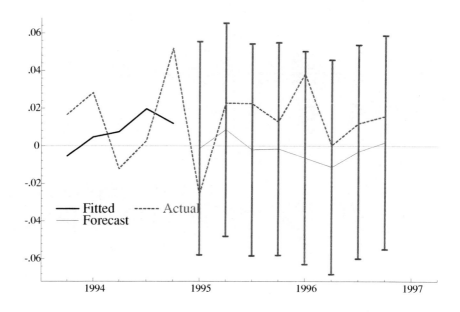

FIGURE C-28: Imports for the U.S.: Predictive Accuracy of the Error-Correction Model

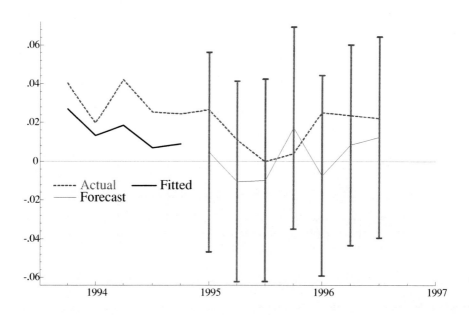

REFERENCES

Ceglowski, Janet, "On the Structural Stability of Trade Equations: The Case of Japan," *Journal of International Money and Finance*, 16 (June 1997), pp. 491–512.

Cline, William R., *United States External Adjustment and the World Economy*, Washington, D.C., Institute for International Economics, 1989.

Deyak, Timothy A., W. Charles Sawyer, and Richard L. Sprinkle, "An Empirical Examination of the Structural Stability of Disaggregated U.S. Import Demand," *Review of Economics and Statistics*, 71 (May 1989), pp. 337–341.

Goldstein, Morris, and Mohsin S. Khan, "Income and Price Effects in Foreign Trade," in Ronald R. Jones and Peter B. Kenen, eds., *Handbook of International Economics*, Vol. 2, Amsterdam and New York, North-Holland, Elsevier, 1985, pp. 1041–1105.

Hendry, David F., and Jurgen Doornik, *PcGive 9.0*, London, International Thomson Business Press, 1996.

Hooper, Peter, "The Stability of Income and Price Elasticities in U.S. Trade, 1975–1977," International Finance Discussion Papers No. 119, Washington, D.C., Board of Governors of the Federal Reserve System, June 1978.

Hooper, Peter, Karen Johnson, and Jaime Marquez, "Trade Elasticities for G-7 Countries," International Finance Discussion Papers No. 609, Washington, D.C., Board of Governors of the Federal Reserve System, April 1998.

Hooper, Peter, and Jaime Marquez, "Exchange Rates, Prices, and External Adjustment in the United States and Japan," in Peter B. Kenen, ed., *Understanding Interdependence*, Princeton N.J., Princeton University Press, 1995, pp. 107–168.

Houthakker, Hendrik S., and Stephen P. Magee, "Income and Price Elasticities in World Trade," *Review of Economics and Statistics*, 51 (May 1969), pp. 111–125.

International Monetary Fund (IMF), *Direction of Trade Statistics*, Yearbook 1996, Washington, D.C., International Monetary Fund, 1996.

———, *International Financial Statistics*, Series REU, Washington, D.C., International Monetary Fund, various issues.

Johansen, Soren, "Statistical Analysis of Cointegration Vectors," *Journal of Economic Dynamics and Control*, 12 (June-September 1988), pp. 231–254.

Krugman, Paul R., "Differences in Income Elasticities and Trends in Real Exchange Rates," *European Economic Review*, 33 (May 1989), pp. 1031–1054.

———, "What Do We Need to Know about the International Monetary System," in Peter B. Kenen, ed., *Understanding Interdependence*, Princeton N.J., Princeton University Press, 1995, pp. 509–529.

Marquez, Jaime, "Bilateral Trade Elasticities," *Review of Economics and Statistics*, 72 (February 1990), pp. 70–77.

———, "Long-Period Trade Elasticities for Canada, Japan, and the United States," *Review of International Economics*, 7 (February 1999), pp. 102–116.

Maskus, Keith E., "Evidence on Shifts in the Determinants of the Structures of U.S. Manufacturing Foreign Trade, 1958–76," *Review of Economics and Statistics*, 65 (August 1983), pp. 415–422.

Sawyer, W. Charles, and Richard L. Sprinkle, "The Demand for Imports and Exports in the U.S.: A Survey," *Journal of Economics and Finance*, 20 (Spring 1996), pp. 147–178.

Stern, Robert M., Christopher Baum, and Mark N. Greene, "Evidence on Structural Change in the Demand for Aggregate U.S. Imports and Exports," *Journal of Political Economy*, 87 (February 1979), pp. 179–192.

Stern, Robert M., Jonathan Francis, and Bruce Schumacher, *Price Elasticities in International Trade: An Annotated Bibliography*, London, Macmillan, 1976.

Zietz, Joachim, and Donald K. Pemberton, "Parameter Instability in Aggregate U.S. Import Demand Functions," *Journal of International Money and Finance*, 12 (December 1993), pp. 654–667.

PUBLICATIONS OF THE
INTERNATIONAL ECONOMICS SECTION

Notice to Contributors

The International Economics Section issues papers in three series. ESSAYS IN INTERNATIONAL ECONOMICS (formerly Essays in International Finance) and PRINCETON STUDIES IN INTERNATIONAL ECONOMICS (formerly Princeton Studies in International Finance) contain new work not published elsewhere. REPRINTS IN INTERNATIONAL ECONOMICS (formerly Reprints in International Finance) reproduce journal articles previously published by Princeton faculty members associated with the Section. A fourth series, SPECIAL PAPERS IN INTERNATIONAL ECONOMICS, was discontinued in July 2000. The Section welcomes the submission of manuscripts for publication under the following guidelines:

ESSAYS are meant to disseminate new views about international economic matters and should be accessible to well-informed nonspecialists as well as to professional economists. Technical terms, tables, and charts should be used sparingly; mathematics should be avoided.

STUDIES are devoted to new research in international economics, with preference given to empirical work. They should be comparable in originality and technical proficiency to papers published in leading economic journals. They should be of medium length, longer than a journal article but shorter than a book.

Manuscripts should be submitted in triplicate, typed single sided and double spaced throughout on 8½ by 11 white bond paper. Publication can be expedited if manuscripts are computer keyboarded in WordPerfect or a compatible program. Additional instructions and a style guide are available from the Section or on the website at www.princeton.edu/~ies.

How to Obtain Publications

The Section's publications are distributed free of charge to college, university, and public libraries and to nongovernmental, nonprofit research institutions. Eligible institutions may ask to be placed on the Section's permanent mailing list.

Individuals and institutions not qualifying for free distribution may receive all publications for the calendar year for a subscription fee of $45.00. Late subscribers will receive all back issues for the year during which they subscribe.

Publications may be ordered individually, with payment made in advance. ESSAYS and REPRINTS cost $10.00 each; STUDIES and SPECIAL PAPERS cost $13.50. An additional $1.50 should be sent for postage and handling within the United States, Canada, and Mexico; $2.25 should be added for surface delivery outside the region.

All payments must be made in U.S. dollars. Subscription fees and charges for single issues will be waived for organizations and individuals in countries where foreign-exchange regulations prohibit dollar payments.

Information about the Section and its publishing program is available at the Section's website at www.princeton.edu/~ies. A subscription and order form is printed at the end of this volume. Correspondence should be addressed to:

International Economics Section
Department of Economics, Fisher Hall
Princeton University
Princeton, New Jersey 08544-1021
Tel: 609-258-4048 • Fax: 609-258-1374
E-mail: ies@princeton.edu

57

List of Recent Publications

A complete list of publications is available at the International Economics Section website at www.princeton.edu/~ies.

ESSAYS IN INTERNATIONAL ECONOMICS
(formerly Essays in International Finance)

180. Warren L. Coats, Jr., Reinhard W. Furstenberg, and Peter Isard, *The SDR System and the Issue of Resource Transfers*. (December 1990)
181. George S. Tavlas, *On the International Use of Currencies: The Case of the Deutsche Mark*. (March 1991)
182. Tommaso Padoa-Schioppa, ed., with Michael Emerson, Kumiharu Shigehara, and Richard Portes, *Europe After 1992: Three Essays*. (May 1991)
183. Michael Bruno, *High Inflation and the Nominal Anchors of an Open Economy*. (June 1991)
184. Jacques J. Polak, *The Changing Nature of IMF Conditionality*. (September 1991)
185. Ethan B. Kapstein, *Supervising International Banks: Origins and Implications of the Basle Accord*. (December 1991)
186. Alessandro Giustiniani, Francesco Papadia, and Daniela Porciani, *Growth and Catch-Up in Central and Eastern Europe: Macroeconomic Effects on Western Countries*. (April 1992)
187. Michele Fratianni, Jürgen von Hagen, and Christopher Waller, *The Maastricht Way to EMU*. (June 1992)
188. Pierre-Richard Agénor, *Parallel Currency Markets in Developing Countries: Theory, Evidence, and Policy Implications*. (November 1992)
189. Beatriz Armendariz de Aghion and John Williamson, *The G-7's Joint-and-Several Blunder*. (April 1993)
190. Paul Krugman, *What Do We Need to Know About the International Monetary System?* (July 1993)
191. Peter M. Garber and Michael G. Spencer, *The Dissolution of the Austro-Hungarian Empire: Lessons for Currency Reform*. (February 1994)
192. Raymond F. Mikesell, *The Bretton Woods Debates: A Memoir*. (March 1994)
193. Graham Bird, *Economic Assistance to Low-Income Countries: Should the Link be Resurrected?* (July 1994)
194. Lorenzo Bini-Smaghi, Tommaso Padoa-Schioppa, and Francesco Papadia, *The Transition to EMU in the Maastricht Treaty*. (November 1994)
195. Ariel Buira, *Reflections on the International Monetary System*. (January 1995)
196. Shinji Takagi, *From Recipient to Donor: Japan's Official Aid Flows, 1945 to 1990 and Beyond*. (March 1995)
197. Patrick Conway, *Currency Proliferation: The Monetary Legacy of the Soviet Union*. (June 1995)
198. Barry Eichengreen, *A More Perfect Union? The Logic of Economic Integration*. (June 1996)
199. Peter B. Kenen, ed., with John Arrowsmith, Paul De Grauwe, Charles A. E. Goodhart, Daniel Gros, Luigi Spaventa, and Niels Thygesen, *Making EMU Happen—Problems and Proposals: A Symposium*. (August 1996)

200. Peter B. Kenen, ed., with Lawrence H. Summers, William R. Cline, Barry Eichengreen, Richard Portes, Arminio Fraga, and Morris Goldstein, *From Halifax to Lyons: What Has Been Done about Crisis Management?* (October 1996)

201. Louis W. Pauly, *The League of Nations and the Foreshadowing of the International Monetary Fund.* (December 1996)

202. Harold James, *Monetary and Fiscal Unification in Nineteenth-Century Germany: What Can Kohl Learn from Bismarck?* (March 1997)

203. Andrew Crockett, *The Theory and Practice of Financial Stability.* (April 1997)

204. Benjamin J. Cohen, *The Financial Support Fund of the OECD: A Failed Initiative.* (June 1997)

205. Robert N. McCauley, *The Euro and the Dollar.* (November 1997)

206. Thomas Laubach and Adam S. Posen, *Disciplined Discretion: Monetary Targeting in Germany and Switzerland.* (December 1997)

207. Stanley Fischer, Richard N. Cooper, Rudiger Dornbusch, Peter M. Garber, Carlos Massad, Jacques J. Polak, Dani Rodrik, and Savak S. Tarapore, *Should the IMF Pursue Capital-Account Convertibility?* (May 1998)

208. Charles P. Kindleberger, *Economic and Financial Crises and Transformations in Sixteenth-Century Europe.* (June 1998)

209. Maurice Obstfeld, *EMU: Ready or Not?* (July 1998)

210. Wilfred Ethier, *The International Commercial System.* (September 1998)

211. John Williamson and Molly Mahar, *A Survey of Financial Liberalization.* (November 1998)

212. Ariel Buira, *An Alternative Approach to Financial Crises.* (February 1999)

213. Barry Eichengreen, Paul Masson, Miguel Savastano, and Sunil Sharma, *Transition Strategies and Nominal Anchors on the Road to Greater Exchange-Rate Flexibility.* (April 1999)

214. Curzio Giannini, *"Enemy of None but a Common Friend of All"? An International Perspective on the Lender-of-Last-Resort Function.* (June 1999)

215. Jeffrey A. Frankel, *No Single Currency Regime Is Right for All Countries or at All Times.* (August 1999)

216. Jacques J. Polak, *Streamlining the Financial Structure of the International Monetary Fund.* (September 1999)

217. Gustavo H. B. Franco, *The Real Plan and the Exchange Rate.* (April 2000)

218. Thomas D. Willett, *International Financial Markets as Sources of Crises or Discipline: The Too Much, Too Late Hypothesis.* (May 2000)

219. Richard H. Clarida, *G-3 Exchange-Rate Relationships: A Review of the Record and of Proposals for Change.* (August 2000)

PRINCETON STUDIES IN INTERNATIONAL ECONOMICS
(formerly Princeton Studies in International Finance)

69. Felipe Larraín and Andrés Velasco, *Can Swaps Solve the Debt Crisis? Lessons from the Chilean Experience.* (November 1990)

70. Kaushik Basu, *The International Debt Problem, Credit Rationing and Loan Pushing: Theory and Experience.* (October 1991)

71. Daniel Gros and Alfred Steinherr, *Economic Reform in the Soviet Union: Pas de Deux*

between Disintegration and Macroeconomic Destabilization. (November 1991)
72. George M. von Furstenberg and Joseph P. Daniels, *Economic Summit Declarations, 1975-1989: Examining the Written Record of International Cooperation*. (February 1992)
73. Ishac Diwan and Dani Rodrik, *External Debt, Adjustment, and Burden Sharing: A Unified Framework*. (November 1992)
74. Barry Eichengreen, *Should the Maastricht Treaty Be Saved?* (December 1992)
75. Adam Klug, *The German Buybacks, 1932-1939: A Cure for Overhang?* (November 1993)
76. Tamim Bayoumi and Barry Eichengreen, *One Money or Many? Analyzing the Prospects for Monetary Unification in Various Parts of the World*. (September 1994)
77. Edward E. Leamer, *The Heckscher-Ohlin Model in Theory and Practice*. (February 1995)
78. Thorvaldur Gylfason, *The Macroeconomics of European Agriculture*. (May 1995)
79. Angus S. Deaton and Ronald I. Miller, *International Commodity Prices, Macroeconomic Performance, and Politics in Sub-Saharan Africa*. (December 1995)
80. Chander Kant, *Foreign Direct Investment and Capital Flight*. (April 1996)
81. Gian Maria Milesi-Ferretti and Assaf Razin, *Current-Account Sustainability*. (October 1996)
82. Pierre-Richard Agénor, *Capital-Market Imperfections and the Macroeconomic Dynamics of Small Indebted Economies*. (June 1997)
83. Michael Bowe and James W. Dean, *Has the Market Solved the Sovereign-Debt Crisis?* (August 1997)
84. Willem H. Buiter, Giancarlo M. Corsetti, and Paolo A. Pesenti, *Interpreting the ERM Crisis: Country-Specific and Systemic Issues*. (March 1998)
85. Holger C. Wolf, *Transition Strategies: Choices and Outcomes*. (June 1999)
86. Alessandro Prati and Garry J. Schinasi, *Financial Stability in European Economic and Monetary Union*. (August 1999)
87. Peter Hooper, Karen Johnson, and Jaime Marquez, *Trade Elasticities for the G-7 Countries*. (August 2000)

SPECIAL PAPERS IN INTERNATIONAL ECONOMICS

17. Richard Pomfret, *International Trade Policy with Imperfect Competition*. (August 1992)
18. Hali J. Edison, *The Effectiveness of Central-Bank Intervention: A Survey of the Literature After 1982*. (July 1993)
19. Sylvester W.C. Eijffinger and Jakob De Haan, *The Political Economy of Central-Bank Independence*. (May 1996)
20. Olivier Jeanne, *Currency Crises: A Perspective on Recent Theoretical Developments*. (March 2000)

REPRINTS IN INTERNATIONAL ECONOMICS
(formerly Reprints in International Finance)

29. Peter B. Kenen, *Sorting Out Some EMU Issues*; reprinted from Jean Monnet Chair Paper 38, Robert Schuman Centre, European University Institute, 1996. (December 1996)

∘ SUBSCRIBE ∘ ORDER ∘

INTERNATIONAL ECONOMICS SECTION

SUBSCRIPTIONS

Rate $45 a year

The International Economics Section issues six to eight publications each year in a mix of Essays, Studies, and occasional Reprints. Late subscribers receive all publications for the subscription year. Prepayment is required and may be made by check in U.S. dollars or by Visa or MasterCard. A complete list of publications is available at www.princeton.edu/~ies.

Address inquiries to:

International Economics Section
Department of Economics, Fisher Hall
Princeton University
Princeton, NJ 08544–1021

BOOK ORDERS

Essays & Reprints $10.00
Studies & Special Papers $13.50

plus postage

Within U.S. $1.50
Outside U.S. (surface mail) $2.25

_____

Discounts are available for book dealers and for orders of five or more publications.

_____

Telephone: 609–258–4048
Telefax: 609–258–1374
E-mail: ies@princeton.edu

INTERNATIONAL ECONOMICS SECTION

This is a subscription ☐ ; a book order ☐

Essay #(s) _____, _____   No. of copies___

Study #(s) _____, _____   No. of copies___

Special Paper # _____   No. of copies ___

Reprint # _____   No. of copies ___

☐ Enclosed is my check made payable to Princeton University, International Economics Section

totaling $_____.

Please charge: ☐ Visa ☐ MasterCard

Acct.# _____

Expires _____

Signature_____

Send to:

Name_____

Address_____

City _____

State _____Zip _____

Country_____

INTERNATIONAL ECONOMICS SECTION
DEPARTMENT OF ECONOMICS
FISHER HALL
PRINCETON UNIVERSITY
PRINCETON, NJ 08544-1021